Poles Apart

Penguin lives at the South Pole.
His best friend, Walrus, lives at
the North Pole. One day they
decide to visit each other.
Find out what happens on their
long journeys.

The front cover

Read the title together: 'Poles Apart'. What could it mean? (*far apart, opposite ends of the Earth*)

Why is the walrus on the North Pole and the penguin on the South Pole?

What do you think it is like at the poles? (*cold, snow, ice, etc.*)

The back cover

Let's read the blurb together.

Where do you think Penguin and Walrus will meet?

Do you recognise what is behind Penguin and Walrus in this picture? (*pyramids in Egypt*)

The title page

Discuss the picture with the children.

Do you know what a compass is and what it is used for?

LESSON 1 (CHAPTER 1)

Read pages 2 and 3

Purpose: To find out facts about the two characters, e.g. who they are, where they live, what they decide to do.

Pause at page 3

Where are Walrus and Penguin at the start of the story? (Use the globe.)

What do they decide to do?

What do you notice about the way the author has written pages 2 and 3? (*Similar structure to show that both animals decide to do the same thing.*)

What do you notice about the pictures? (*part-cartoon, part-photograph*)

Read pages 4 and 5

Purpose: To find out what Walrus did.

Pause at page 5

What does page 4 tell you about what Walrus did? Does the postcard tell you anything more? Do you think the author is using the postcard to tell some of the story?

Look at the postcard. Point out the postcard features. (*postcard shape, stamp, postmark, address*)

Tricky word (page 4):
The word 'sleigh' may be beyond the children's word recognition skills. Tell this word to the children.

Walrus lived on the cold ice at the
North Pole.

One day Walrus said, "I would love to
go and see my friend Penguin."

So Walrus left his home and set off
on the long journey to the South Pole.

2

Penguin lived on the cold ice at the
South Pole.

On the very same day Penguin said,
"I would love to go and see my
friend Walrus."

So Penguin left her home and set off
on the long journey to the North Pole.

3

Walrus had not gone far when he met some
huskies. They took him for a ride in a sleigh.
Walrus was so excited that he sent a postcard
to Penguin.

4

5

READ

Read pages 6 and 7

Purpose: To find out where Penguin is.

EXPLORE

Pause at page 7

Where is Penguin? Who does she meet and what do they do?

Find the word 'Meanwhile' on page 6. What does it mean? Re-read the sentence with expression.

Compare Penguin's postcard on page 7 with Walrus's postcard on page 5, and discuss how they are similar.

READ

Read pages 8 to 11

Purpose: To find out where Walrus and Penguin go next.

Tricky word (page 6):
The word 'Australia' may be beyond the children's word recognition skills. Tell this word to the children.

Tricky word (page 8):
The word 'Hawaii' may also want to be discussed as a tricky word.

Meanwhile, Penguin was in Australia.
She met some friendly kangaroos. They
showed her how to jump. Penguin was so
excited that she sent a postcard to Walrus.

Meanwhile, Walrus swam and swam
until he came to Hawaii. He met some
people on the beach. They put a garland
of flowers around his neck and showed
him how to dance.

Walrus couldn't wait to tell
Penguin, so he sent her a postcard.

Pause at page 11

What happened to Penguin in China?

What happened to Walrus in Hawaii?

Look at all the postcards and comment on the stamps and artefacts on the corners of the postcards. Where are they from? What do they tell us?

Read pages 12 and 13

Purpose: To find out what the parrot said to Walrus.

Pause at page 13

What is happening in the conversation between Walrus and the parrot? (*the parrot is mimicking what Walrus says*)

Does Walrus like it in the rain forest? What sentences tell you this? (*I am too hot, I miss my nice ice*)

Look at 'were here' and 'nice ice'. Do you notice anything about these words? (*Two sets of words with similar spelling, but one set rhymes, other doesn't.*)

Please turn to page 14 for Revisit and Respond activities.

Meanwhile, Penguin travelled on.
She came to China. She saw a wonderful
firework display and a dancing dragon.
Penguin sent Walrus a postcard.

Walrus came to a rain forest in Brazil,
where he met a parrot.
"I am too hot," said Walrus.
"I am too hot," said the parrot.
"I miss my nice ice," said Walrus.
"I miss my nice ice," said the parrot.
"Good-bye," said Walrus.
"Good-bye," said the parrot.
Walrus sent a postcard to Penguin.

LESSON 2

Recap lesson 1

Why is the story called 'Poles Apart'?

Where are Walrus and Penguin going in this story?

Where have they been? Who have they met?

What do they always send one another?

Read pages 14 and 15

Purpose: To trace Penguin's and Walrus's journeys.

Pause at page 15

Check the children understand what this map shows.

What route has Penguin taken so far in the book? (*Prompt children to point out the route, saying what happened where.*) What route has Walrus taken so far? Where are they both going?

Read pages 16 to 21

Purpose: To find out if Penguin and Walrus meet and where.

Tricky word (page 14):
The word 'Egypt' may be beyond the children's word recognition skills. Tell this word to the children.

Tricky word (page 16):
The word 'pyramids' may also want to be discussed as a tricky word.

Walrus and Penguin travelled over land
and sea until they came to Egypt.

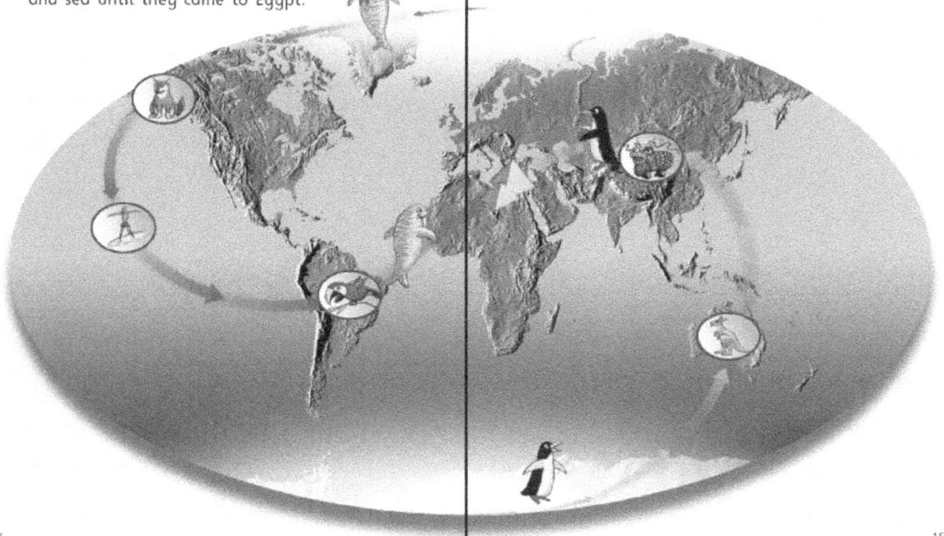

14

15

Walrus went to look at the pyramids.
Penguin went to look at the pyramids.
Then they met!
"Walrus, it's you!" laughed Penguin.
"Penguin, it's you!" laughed Walrus.
They were so happy to see each other.

Then they had some
adventures together.
They had a ride on a
train – a camel train!

16

17

9

Pause at page 21

Where do Penguin and Walrus meet?

What do they get up to in Egypt?

What words tell you they were very pleased to see each other? (*laughed, so happy*) (page 16)

What phrase do Walrus and Penguin use to show their enjoyment. (*'This is the life'*)

What does a 'camel train' mean? (page 17)

Which river do they ride down?

Discuss the mix of cartoons and photographs on pages 16 to 21.

They visited a museum.
Walrus learned another dance.

After that, to cool off, they had a ride
down the River Nile.
"This is the life," said Penguin.
"This is the life," said Walrus.

Read pages 22 to the end

Purpose: To predict the ending and see if you are right.

Pause at page 23

Why do Walrus and Penguin want to go home? (*It's too hot for them in Egypt.*)

What does Walrus say that shows this? ('*I miss my nice ice*')

Why did Walrus and Penguin have so many postcards waiting for them at home?

What was the theme of the story? (*Two friends making a long journey to see each other.*)

What would have happened if the two friends had not met in Egypt? (*They would have completely missed each other.*)

Why is this a circular story? (*It ends where it began.*)

Soon, it was time to say good-bye. Walrus
wanted to go home to the North Pole.
Penguin wanted to go home to the South Pole.
"I miss my nice ice," said Walrus.
"Me too," said Penguin.

Walrus went home to the North Pole.
"What a lot of postcards from Penguin!"
he said. He sent another postcard to Penguin.

Penguin went home to the South Pole.
"What a lot of postcards from Walrus," she
said. She sent another postcard to Walrus.

After Reading
Revisit and Respond

Lesson 1

- What part do the postcards play in the story? (*they make the story interesting, they tell the story from Walrus's or Penguin's point of view*)

- What information about the countries can you get from the postcards? (*stamps, artefacts, etc.*)

- Ask the children to find words in the story so far with capital letters, and list them as (a) words that start a sentence, (b) names of characters and (c) names of places.

Lesson 2

- Ask the children to write a postcard from Britain, or another place they have visited, as though they are Walrus writing to Penguin.

- Discuss what things to include in a postcard, i.e. opening and closing salutations, the address and postcard-style phrasing, (e.g. *Wish you were here*).

- Discuss how the story structure changes when the friends meet (i.e. there are no postcards).

- Ask the children to do a role-play of the story, with one child playing Penguin, the other Walrus. They should read only what is said on the postcards. Ask the others to identify how well the story is told and what parts are missing (e.g. *where they met*).

- Ask the children if Walrus seems realistic as a character. Why?

- Write a list of the places that Walrus and Penguin visited, and choose adjectives to describe each.

Follow-up

Independent Group Activity Work

This book is accompanied by two photocopy masters, one with a reading focus, and one with a writing focus, which support the teaching objectives of this book. The photocopy masters can be found in the Planning and Assessment Guide.

PCM F6.1 (*reading*)

PCM F6.2 (*writing*)

You may also like to invite the children to read the text again during their independent reading (either at school or at home).

Writing

Guided writing: Write a postcard inviting Walrus to your home. Try to persuade him what a good place it would be to visit.

Extended writing: Write about what Penguin would do if she came to visit you.

Assessment Points

Assess that the children have learnt the main teaching points of the book by checking that they can:

- engage with books through exploring and enacting interpretations (e.g. use of role play).